The
Quest
for
Serenity

The Quest for Serenity

G. H. Morling

With introduction, notes, and commentary by

Ruth Bell Graham

WORD PUBLISHING
Dallas · London · Sydney · Singapore

THE QUEST FOR SERENITY

By G. H. Morling, with notes and commentary by Ruth Bell Graham

Every effort has been made to trace ownership of copyrighted material used in this book and to secure permission for its use. Should there be any inadvertent error or omission, the publisher will be pleased to make the necessary corrections in future printings. Grateful acknowledgment is made for permission to quote the following selections:

"For All People" (p. 5) from HALFWAY UP THE SKY by Jane Merchant. Copyright renewal ©1985 by Elizabeth Merchant. Used by permission of the publisher, Abingdon Press.

"For the One Who Is Tired" (p. 57), from SONGS OF HOPE by Grace Noll Crowell. Copyright 1938 by Harper & Row, Publishers, Inc. Renewal copyright © 1966 by Grace Noll Crowell. Reprinted by permission of Harper & Row, Publishers, Inc.

"Before the winds that blow do cease" (p. 67) from *Edges of His Ways* by Amy Carmichael, copyright 1955 Dohnavur Fellowship (London: S.P.C.K.; Ft. Washington, PA: Christian Literature Crusade). Used by permission.

Scripture quotations in this book are from the King James Version of the Bible.

Library of Congress Cataloging-in-Publication Data:

Morling, G. H.
  The quest for serenity.

1. Peace of mind—Religious aspects—Christianity.
I. Graham, Ruth Bell. II. Title.
BV4908.5.M67 1989   248.4   89-5307
ISBN 0-8499-0676-8

Printed in the United States of America

9 8 0 1 2 3 9 AGK 9 8 7 6 5 4 3 2 1

TO MY WIFE
*to whom I owe
the blessing of
a restful home*

FOR ALL PEOPLE . . .

God bless
   and fortify them
God hear
   when they entreat
The strong
   courageous people
Too brave
   to own defeat

And Oh,
   God bless and help them
God answer
   when they call
The tired
   defeated people
Who are not
   brave at all.

—Jane Merchant

Contents

"Now therefore, our God, the great, the mighty, and the terrible God . . . let not all the weariness seem little before thee, that hath come upon us" (Nehemiah 9:32, note).

Introduction

NECESSITY SEEMS to have been laid upon me to write this book. In that fact lies my chief hope that some will find in it an authentic word of God.

The book is a personal testimony of faith and experience. Its unity is not mainly that of logical development but rather that of life history.

I have interpreted rest as being oceanic in character. Therefore I have written much more in terms of principles than of rules. Obviously, limitations of space have greatly embarrassed me: I should like to have had opportunity to develop much of what I have written.

I express thanks to a small group of friends who have helped me greatly in the preparation of these pages. I count myself fortunate in these friendships.

G.H.M.

"Thou hast lifted me up, and hast not made my foes to rejoice over me" (Psalm 30:1).

An Additional Word

By
Ruth Bell
Graham

"WE LIVE in tension, then, and the tension is what keeps us alive?" someone asked Dr. Paul Tournier, the noted Swiss psychiatrist.

Tournier replied, "And it is what keeps him young. . . . The people who are the most alive are those who are the most torn."*

Victor Frankl made a similar statement in *Man's Search for Meaning*: "Mental health is based on a certain amount of tension. . . . What man actually needs is not a tensionless state but rather the striving and struggling for some goal worthy of him.

"If architects want to strengthen a decrepit arch, they increase the load which is laid upon it, for thereby the parts are joined more firmly together."

Yet pressure and tension do not preclude serenity, as Paul Tournier pointed out elsewhere. This fact is demonstrated clearly and simply in the earthly life of Jesus—a life of peace and calm amid tremendous pressures.

It is resentment and fretting—not tension—that rob us of the serenity we need. Someone has said we are not responsible for events, only for our reactions

*From an interview with Paul Tournier in *Christian Herald*, September 1965.

"Consider the continual war which prevails among men even in times of peace, and which exists not only between nations and countries and cities, but also between private houses, or, I might say, is present with every individual man; observe the unspeakable raging storm in men's souls that is excited by the violent rush of the affairs of life; and you may well wonder whether anyone can enjoy tranquility in such a storm, and maintain calm amidst the surge of this billowing sea."

William Barclay

to them. When we react to events with resentment and bitterness, we pay an enormous price physically, mentally, spiritually, and emotionally.

Yet reacting receptively can be difficult for those of us who have flaws in our personalities and characters, inherited by birth or acquired as children from events or associations beyond our control, that predispose us to wear ourselves out with worry and cares. It can be deeply disturbing to find oneself reacting the wrong way out of inability to react in any other. How do we develop the inner peace and serenity we so desperately need?

G. H. Morling addresses this problem better and more simply than anyone I know. Perhaps, having been there himself, he understands that the tired mind can only grasp the simple truths, simply put— and tired hands do not need to hold heavy books. And so he has kept his book small, easy to read, and right to the point.

Amy Carmichael of India found in her twenty years of physical illness that most of the books for the ill were written by the well. So she wrote one of her best books, the classic *Rose from Briar*, as from "one ill person to another."

And Morling has done the same for us—sharing out of the personal depths through which he passed practical suggestions and words of timeless help. He writes as one person who finds serenity elusive to those of us who also struggle in this area.

This little volume, written from the depths of Morling's personal experience, has helped countless thousands of people. Certainly it has been a treasure to me over these years. My copy has grown worn and dog-eared as I have taken notes in it, marked its pages, and fattened it with scraps of paper containing quotes, poems, articles.

"God is a tranquil Being, and abides in a tranquil eternity. So must thy spirit become a tranquil and clear little pool, wherein the serene light of God can be mirrored. Therefore shun all that is disquieting and distracting, both within and without. Nothing in the whole world is worth the loss of thy peace; even the faults which thou has committed should only humble, but not disquiet them. God is full of joy, peace, and happiness. Endeavor then to obtain a continually joyful and peaceful spirit. Avoid all anxious care, vexation, murmuring, and melancholy, which darken thy soul and render thee unfit for the friendship of God. If thou dost perceive such feelings arising, turn gently away from them."

Gerhardt Tersteegen

When we realized that Morling's book was no longer available to the public, we sought to have it brought back into print. So here you have Morling's text exactly as he wrote it, with the addition of some notes I have made and some of the additional material I have collected over the years.

I hope my comments and quotations will not be intrusive. They are just bits and pieces that have helped me down through the years. But more important, I hope that Morling's timeless little book will be a source of peace and help to you in tense and troubled times of life, as that is when they have helped me most.

RUTH BELL GRAHAM

1

Introduction to the Quest

"Let not mine enemies triumph over me" (Psalm 25:2). See also Psalm 13.

1

THE HISTORIAN tells us that there was a remarkable modernness about the world in which Jesus lived. It was a world modern in social habit; men traveled for pleasure, or business, or education, using, on land, excellently constructed highways. It was modern in the conduct of business; there was a highly developed banking system with letters of credit and bills of exchange provided. There were strangely up-to-date amenities; postal services were common and the Romans had something akin to our daily newspaper. A hot air system was in use in the first century B.C. Dentistry was practiced; teeth were actually filled with gold. And vice was the same; there were dishonorable get-rich-quick schemes, gambling was widespread, immorality and racial suicide reached alarming proportions, luxury and extravagance were rife even to the extent of feasting on the brains of peacocks and the tongues of nightingales.

More especially was that ancient world modern in its essential spirit; it was a deeply disturbed world. Restlessness had invaded it just as it has ours. That air of disturbance appears in a literature in which skepticism and superstition, in true present-day fashion, exhaust themselves and issue in despair. It found a more poignant expression. On tombstones unearthed in Asia Minor are found inscriptions in which the bereaved pour out their sorrow. Here are engraven the heartache of desolate parents who will

> "They would rejoice over us if they could keep us cast down. It would be so evident then that we had a hard master; that things are not as He had promised they would be; that peace could not be continual; that we could not hope for more than to go on stumbling on our way depressed and depressing, far, far from being more than conquerors through Him that loved us."
>
> Amy Wilson Carmichael

hear no more the patter of little feet, and the yearning of widow and widower for the beloved dead. And all are without hope for, as yet, life and immortality had not been brought to light. Into that restless world came One Who, knowing its unspeakable need, still dared to call Himself the Rest Giver.

One day in Galilee, it may have been as evening shadows were falling and men turned homewards from their heavy toil, Our Lord Jesus stood looking into wistful faces that bore manifest marks of weariness. With the insight of love, Jesus knew that the tiredness was not merely physical but was much more a total life exhaustion. Stirred to pity, that Lover of men uttered the most gracious words that have ever fallen on the hungry heart of humanity. "Come unto me all ye that labor and are heavyladen," He cried, "and I will give you rest."

I have entitled this book, *The Quest for Serenity*. I might almost have entitled it *My Quest for Serenity* because in it I have set down the results of my own deliberate and prolonged seeking after inner quiet. The quest has been by no means easy. I carried from childhood into riper years a legacy of nervous weakness. In early years I was beset with debilitating fears. There were the usual distresses associated with a highly sensitive nature; and there were others beyond the ordinary. I had eerie experiences of going off into nothingness which filled nights with dread.

In his tender years the poet Wordsworth used sometimes to grasp a fence in order to assure himself that he was real. In the light of my own childhood I can readily account for such an action. The child is father of the man. I emerged into normal physically healthy youth and manhood, and tendencies to nervous unbalance remained.

"I heard the voice of Jesus say,
'Come unto Me and rest;
Lay down, thou weary one, lay down
Thy head upon My breast.'
I came to Jesus as I was,
Weary, and worn, and sad;
I found in Him a resting place,
And He has made me glad."

Horatius Bonar

Life education for me has meant largely the control and correction of these elements of my inheritance. Out of sheer necessity I had to undertake a quest for serenity. Simply I tell that, in my quest, I myself came to the Divine Rest Giver. Enthusiastically I declare that, in Livingstone's great phrase, He is "of the most immaculate honor." Thankfully I relate that my quest has not been fruitless. I have, by no means, fully attained it; I am not already perfect in serenity. But, because I have had a greater need than most, being myself compassed with infirmity, I might be able, with the good hand of God upon me, to be a humble helper in your own quest for serenity. So let us to the high adventure.

To the restlessness of that ancient world did Jesus announce Himself as the Rest Giver. His invitation extends to the restless of our day; for He is the Eternal Contemporary. It is the purpose of these pages to unfold the meaning of the invitation.

"In the world ye shall have pressure, [literal Greek translation] but be of good cheer, I have overcome the world" (John 16:33).

The word for pressure, Barclay tells us, is the word used for sheer, unbearable, crushing, physical weight. Like that which they used in ancient times to crush a man to death.

" . . . I cannot read. I cannot
    pray.
I cannot even think.
Where to from here? and how
    get there
with only darkness everywhere?
I ought to rise and only
    sink. . . .
and feel His arms, and hear
    Him say,
'I love you.' . . . It was all my
    soul
or body needed to be whole."

Ruth Bell Graham
"The Little Things That Bug Me"
In *Sitting by My Laughing Fire*

2

The Calm of Sins Forgiven

"'Forgiven!' one brief glimpse
  He gave;
  'Twas all that I could bear;
Enough to bring me to His
    feet—
  Enough to keep me there.
For then the shadows of my
  heart
  By His own hands were riven,
As on its darkest page He wrote
  One shining word,
    'Forgiven!'"

Edith Gilling Cherry

2

OUR FIRST BUSINESS in the quest is plainly to get a sense of direction. We must not be like the man who "sprang into the saddle and rode rapidly in all directions!" That sense of direction will be determined by the explanation which we give to human unrest. I know that there are proximate answers which have to do with external conditions of life such as economic insecurity, international tensions; and with the constitution of our mysterious minds such as unhealthy repressions and the conflict of instincts. I do not underestimate the importance of these answers. But my concern is not with the proximate but with the ultimate.

Let us clearly understand, therefore, that, in the last analysis, man's unrest is traceable to the upsurge within him of desires and dissatisfactions, of hopes and fears, of sorrows, of shames that take their rise in the unfathomable depths of his being. For man has *a sense of timelessness*. The Hebrew Sage wrote significantly, "Thou has set eternity in his heart."* He suggests that, though man's feet are set in a world of time, he yet has intimations of the eternal so that life has an atmosphere of mystery which, unrelieved, disturbs to the point of distress. Many a sensitive soul has felt that eternity murmurs on life's horizons.

*Ecclesiastes 3:11 (Hebrew).

And, more specifically, man has a *sense of the Divine*. As a bird has an instinct that takes it to its distant nest, so has man a home instinct for God that does not allow him ever to be more than a stranger and pilgrim on the earth. And unsatisfied home hunger spells restlessness.

It is of interest that recent research into the fact of personality has tended strongly to confirm the testimony of the Holy Scriptures that God is "our dwelling place." We are told that to investigate the question, "Who am I?" is to be taken up into a "cosmic task"; that to be a "self" is impossible without being united to a wider consciousness; that finiteness is meaningless except by reference to the infinite, so that our life is always hid in a deeper life: that a person is a being who is not a "bare self" but one who in his strivings and seekings is rooted and grounded in a larger self.

Thus it is that man hungers for God and is never really at rest until he finds God. George Borrow relates that, in one of his journeys, he met with a band of gypsies, with whom he spent some time in friendly conversation. He was amazed to hear their aged leader say after a time, "O Sir, we want God. Can you give us God?" Borrow, in his embarrassment, tried to turn the conversation into other channels and finally gave the children money as he prepared to depart. "Sir, we don't want your money," persisted the gypsy. "Can't you give us God?" The cry of the needy heart is not often as articulate as that, but the need is always present and is one element in the ultimate explanation of man's unrest.

Closely related is *the sense of sin*. The sense of sin also takes us into the realm of the ultimate. Nothing is as disturbing as that. Undoubtedly, in recent years, there has been a weakening of the sense of sin; but the sense remains even though its expression is not so obvious. Some three or four decades ago Sir Oliver Lodge said that "men are not worrying about their sins today." In the intervening years sin has become still more blatant.

Yet acute observers interpret the situation differently. Instead they hold that the desperate disorders of society have their roots in the efforts of sin-burdened people to escape from themselves. Moreover, being what he is, man is never immune from the invasion of a sense of guilt. "Guilt," says Hartmann, "bursts in upon man like a fate. It is suddenly there, judging, contradicting, overpowering . . . something over which he has no power."

Men and women without God are restless because they are made in the image of God, Who is their home, and are fundamentally unhappy in the homelessness of a life away from Him and in the consciousness of sin, which either brings in its train distressing fear or else leads to escapist habits of life in which there is no promise of rest.

That is the diagnosis of human unrest. In the light of it we can see clearly the direction which our quest for serenity must take. The rest for which we crave is, first of all, the "calm of sins forgiven." It is plain, also, that no human guide can take us into that desired haven, but only One Who is much more can guide. The psychologist, of himself, cannot, for the trouble is not mainly psychological but moral. Neither does the philosopher suffice, for we need not only light but resources. Here, too, the practical man fails us with his excellent commonsense. The problem is in the realms of the spirit quite out of his reach. But the Lord Jesus does give rest. Let us see what that ministry is by which He speaks peace to the homeless and the burdened.

"A well known British physician is quoted as saying 90% of the patients in mental hospitals could be released if only they could get rid of a sense of guilt."

Paul Tournier

THE CALM OF
SINS FORGIVEN

It is, in part, a ministry of *revelation*. The Lord Jesus came, showing us what God is like so that, knowing Him as He really is, we should not be afraid to go to Him "weak and sinful tho' we be."

The revelation must needs be through the medium of incarnation. There is deep significance in a story told by Dr. Rufus Jones, the notable Quaker philosopher. When a mother assured her little daughter that she need not be afraid of the dark, because God was with her, the child answered, "But I don't want God; I want someone with a face." The child spoke for all of us. We all want someone with a face. Because of that want, the Word became flesh and dwelt among us. Ever since, man has been able to see the glory of God in the face of Jesus Christ. And what a revelation it is. The final truth of the incarnation is plainly this: that God is just like Jesus. Did not the Incarnate One Himself plainly say so in His words, "He that hath seen Me hath seen the Father"?* Is there not the great supporting statement that the Son is the "outshining of God's glory and the exact reproduction of His person"?

The wonder of that revelation was brought home to me most vividly during a visit to India. One Sunday morning in Comilla I saw a man wearing the scarlet thread of the Brahman, carrying his little daughter to the Christian Sunday School. Previously I had seen the Kali Temple in which the father served, a temple hideous with idols, some ludicrous, some cruel, some foul. The little one had been taught at home that God was like those idolatrous representations. Now she was to be told the sweet story of Jesus, the Emmanuel, God with us. I realized, as

*John 14:9.

never before, the glory of the revelation that God is just like Jesus.

Thus was the Divine Rest Giver a revealer, as a rest giver must needs be.

His was also a ministry of *invitation*. It was part of His ministry to invite men and women to return to God. The invitation was given urgently. The Lord Jesus told people that God wanted them even more than they wanted Him. One day some Jewish teachers openly sneered because they saw Him in the company of undesirable characters. His answer was given in the form of three parables—The Lost Sheep, The Lost Coin, The Lost Son—all of which enforce the same truth: that there is distress in the heart of God while lost souls are away from Him. "You scoff because I am with these outcasts," He said in effect. "I will tell you why I do it. These are men away from a God Who feels the loss of them as much as a shepherd who has only a hundred sheep feels the loss of one of the small flock; as much as a woman the loss of one of the ten pieces of silver that compose a cherished adornment which is the gift of her bridegroom; as much as a father the loss of one of his two sons." One of a hundred; one of ten; one of two. A sheep; a precious personal possession; a son. In such rising intensity did Jesus reveal the passion of God for the lost.

There are those who maintain that, having thus disclosed the heart of God and assured sinners of a Heavenly Father's welcome, Jesus had nothing more to do to effect the home-going of the soul. Just as there never was anything except his own unwillingness to prevent the Prodigal from going home, so, it is urged, there never has been anything except the sinner's own refusal or reluctance to keep him away from God.

"Come ye sinners, poor and
   needy,
  Weak and wounded, sick and
   sore;
Jesus ready stands to save you,
  Full of pity, love, and power.

*   *   *

Let not conscience make you
   linger,
  Nor of fitness fondly dream;
All the fitness He requireth
  Is to feel your need of Him."

Joseph Hart

Illustration: Mother of thirteen who, when asked which one she loved the most, thought a moment and replied, "The one who is sick until he is well and the one who is lost, until he is found."

27

But there is much more than that to be said. It was competent for the father in the parable simply to forgive and receive; because offenses against man are only personal in character. But God is God and not man. Offenses against Him are not only offenses against a person, but against the moral law which must be safeguarded if there is not to be moral anarchy. Sin not only hurts the heart of God: it also disturbs the ethical order. So it is that the yearning love of God cannot release itself in forgiveness until the demands of the violated holiness of God, of which the moral law is an expression, are satisfied. And if it be objected that this exalts law above God, we answer God *is* the moral law. In Him "the law is alive." No other doctrine takes the torment out of this guilty conscience. James Denney, himself in the first rank of Scottish scholarship, once said, "Some scholars say they cannot understand these things. But, what of that? If scholars cannot, sinners can. And Jesus did not die for scholars, but for sinners."

It is by such considerations that we come to understand that the Divine Rest Giver must needs have not only a ministry of revelation and of invitation but also of *salvation*, in which His atoning death is central. So it is that He must die before He could bring us to God. Not that Jesus must die to save us from God; but rather that God in Christ must "take sides with us against Himself," before His love could flow out unhindered in welcoming the sinner home! So the Son of God died a death which was "appalling midnight in the soul, the horror of a great darkness, abandonment—the Father's house obscured, the Father's hand vanished, and the Son of God out there in the night in the outer darkness, in the agonies of a consuming loneliness."

Thus the Lord Jesus has met the deepest needs of man's hungry heart; and is able to minister rest to us.

These things have been effected: (1) He gives a satisfying vision of God to the heart which is burdened by the unsolved riddle of the universe.

(2) He relieves the conscience of the sense of guilt. Men who come to the Christ of Calvary are vividly conscious that their sins are forgiven for His sake, and that the moral problem created by their sin has vanished. Now they are properly adjusted to an ethical universe with which their spiritual experience is consistent.

(3) He takes us home to God. Just as the weary child lays its head on the mother's breast and whispers, "That is what I wanted," so the soul, not only forgiven but also accepted in the Beloved, is able to repose in the heart of God with its last longing satisfied.

To us it is that Jesus thus speaks peace. He speaks peace because He *is* our peace. He is our peace because He has made peace through the blood of His Cross. All of which means that the Divine Rest Giver is, first of all, Savior. Dora Greenwell was entirely right when she wrote:

> He did not come to judge the world,
>   He did not come to blame:
> He did not only come to seek—it was to
>   save He came:
> And when we call Him Saviour, then we
>   call Him by His name.

3

Faith's Deepening Rest

"Remember this, busy and
burdened disciple; man or
woman tried by uncertain health;
immersed in secular duties;
forced to a life of almost ceaseless
publicity. Here is written . . . a
guarantee, that not only at holy
times and welcome intervals only,
not only in the dust of death, but
in the dust of life, there is
prepared for you the peace of
God, able to keep your hearts and
thoughts in Christ Jesus. . . . It
is the secret of His presence.
Amidst the circumstances of your
life, which are the expression of
His will, He can keep you in it.
Nay . . . 'shall keep,' alive, and
loving, and practical, and ready at
His call."

Handley C. G. Moule

3

THERE IS not only an unrest of unbelief. There is also an unrest of deficient belief. In our quest for serenity we must take serious account of the second sort as of the first.

The soul that comes to the Savior hears the blood of Jesus whisper peace within; but that glad coming is not without possibilities of new life disturbances. We cannot remain in the company of that Glorious One without sharing His ideals and having aspirations aroused to realize them. Friendship with the great and noble of earth is always exacting; how much more friendship with Jesus Christ, Who is not only Friend but Lord.

Ideals and aspirations are always disturbing. At first, they may be sweetly disturbing; later, unless there are resources adequate for their fulfillment, they can lead on to a painful sense of frustration, even to despair. The lives of great servants of God give ample evidence of this. Biography makes it abundantly clear that there is an unrest of the saint even as there is an unrest of the sinner. Sometimes there is an undefined sense of spiritual need. At an early stage of his Christian life, Thomas Cook was conscious of "a mighty want, a vacuum which grace has not filled, a strange sense of need."

Here is a statement of a more explicit kind concerning a known spiritual deficiency. Mrs. Howard Taylor has written thus about her early years in China:

"The nearer you get to heaven the closer to hell you'll feel."

Samuel Rutherford

FAITH'S
DEEPENING REST

"When I went out to China it was with real consecration to God, and real desire to live for Him only, but out there in China I came to see that there was a great lack in my life. I was often out of touch with the Lord Jesus, often weary, hungry and longing for blessing. From the first day I landed in China, God began to show me my need by humbling me in the dust. He brought me in contact with other lives that were what I wanted to be."

Mother Eva of Friedenshort has written in terms of unsuccessful combat: "Struggling, striving, fighting, I was always painfully conscious that I was not rising to God's ideals in my life. Neither outward poverty nor the daily opportunity for loving service could silence the tumult in my soul, and often a deep sigh arose from my heart: Is this all? Has God nothing now to give me?" Handley Moule said he was "just hungry for some gracious thing if it is to be found." Joseph Brice sums up such testimonies as "the undeniable need of Something Better."

And there is something more. More fundamental than the sense of deficiency and defeat and futility is the consciousness of inner defilement. In the presence of God's Holy Child, Jesus, Peter was constrained to say, "Depart from me, for I am a sinful man, O Lord." Often has the heavenly vision called forth a similar confession of inner uncleanness. We see ourselves when we see the Holy One.

All through the ages the saints have literally sobbed about the sin resident in their hearts. "My heart is the very dunghill of the devil, and it is no easy work to wrestle with him on his own ground," said Jacob Behmen. "My heart is a cage of unclean beasts!" cried a mediaeval saint. "I am made of sin," lamented Bishop Andrewes.

Job: "I have heard of thee by the hearing of the ear; but now mine eye seeth thee: Wherefore I abhor myself, and repent in dust and ashes" (Job 42:5).

It is not, however, the fact of indwelling sin that causes the saints distress so much as inability to deal with it.

In the first flush of the joy of his conversion the young Spurgeon was transported to the heavenly places and felt himself "an emancipated soul, an heir of heaven, forgiven, accepted in Christ, plucked from the miry clay, his feet set upon a rock, and his going established." But, even so, after a few weeks he records that "certain follies had begun to sprout again. . . . My soul seems to long after the flesh pots of Egypt, and that, after having eaten of heavenly manna. Help and forgive me, our Saviour."

Still more penetrating is the testimony of Oswald Chambers: "The sense of depravity and the bad-motiveness of my nature was terrific. I knew no one who had what I wanted. In fact, I did not know what I did want, but I knew that if what I had was all the Christianity there was, then the thing was a mockery."

So if the believer in Jesus Christ is to live serenely he must have Something Better, some Gracious thing which will supply deficiency and correct uncleanness, and there is this Greater Beyond to which the new distress leads, for the purpose of attaining which, indeed the Heavenly Father allows the distress; for, as Madame Guyon found in her similar afflictions, "destruction in the spiritual experience turns to renovation, that out of the sorrows and silences of inward crucifixion and from no other source, must grow the jubilees."

And there is Something Better. The older theologians used to speak about the distinction between our standing and our state, the one having to do with a divine righteousness *imputed*, issuing in justification, the other with a divine righteousness *imparted*, issuing in sanctification. The Something Better is bound up with the knowledge of, and the response to, all that is comprehended with the divine righteousness which is imparted. Paul speaks of a "righteousness of God revealed from faith to faith." If faith does not advance to lay hold of this second aspect of righteousness, which is nothing less than the holiness of God resident within the regenerated heart, then the Heavenly Father cannot satisfy the longing soul.

It is not enough to have God's gift of pardoning grace which, as a robe of righteousness, covers the sinful life. The sinful life must itself become righteous. Justifying righteousness brings only peace of conscience and the cessation of fear regarding the eternal future. It declares a divine amnesty and gives a title to heaven.

We need more than that; and, in the opulence of grace there is something more, much more. There is sanctifying righteousness which, from within, transforms the life. If the one secures our title to heaven, the other procures our fitness for it and, in so doing, floods it with radiance.

In enlarging upon the culture of the inner life I venture to make reference to my own spiritual pilgrimage. In my own life, increase of rest has kept pace with deeper insight into the doctrines of grace which minister to the life within. There came a time in young manhood when, although I was a sincere and outwardly loyal disciple, doubts and fears assailed me. Then I "walked in darkness and knew no light"; however, I could and did still trust in the name of the Lord and stay upon my God.

The dawning of a great light was not far off. The Sunrising from on high soon visited me. I became assured of sonship with God and I have never for a moment wavered in that assurance. I could now fight with my feet shod with the preparation of the Gospel of peace. That meant much.

But I, too, needed and wanted the Something Better. Service was rendered to the Lord Jesus and His Church with an almost intolerable sense of strain. There was a burdensome sensitiveness and a great anxiety about results.

Relief came, as through patient study and prayer, enlightenment was given on God's provisions for a naturally restless heart like mine. As, one by one, the magnificent truths of grace were brought home to me, I made humble heart adjustment to them. There have been no cataclysmic experiences; only a progressively enriched experience. George Macdonald has said suggestively that one can have an impoverished experience by living on experiences.

In this process of enlightenment, first of all there was brought under my notice, vividly and repeatedly, the truth of "the Soul's union with Christ." I can still remember the thrill, both intellectual and spiritual, with which I received it. I rejoiced to learn that, as a believer, I was joined to my Lord in a holy union of love; that I was in Christ and that Christ was in me; that no union on earth was more real than this mystic union with Christ.

In the possession of this scriptural doctrine I found a potent secret of inner control. I saw that because of Christ's indwelling I had Christ's own life within me, a life which had known experience on earth and, though tempted in all points such as we are, had been without sin. Under the guidance of wise masters of the inner life, I adopted a new spiritual technique. I stopped praying for my own self to be controlled. Instead I prayed for grace to cease

"Lord Jesus, make Thyself to me
A living bright reality,
More present to faith's vision
    keen
Than any earthly object seen.
More sweet, more intimately
    nigh
Than e'en the sweetest earthly
    tie."

Author unknown

from myself, and to allow Christ to live His own life through me.

Instead of praying in times of stress, "Lord, keep me calm," I prayed, "Lord, entrench me in Thy calm. Not now my weakness made strong but my weakness abandoned and Thy strength, a strength tested and triumphant in like circumstances, permitted to express itself through my surrendered personality."

That was gain indeed. It was not only an immediate enrichment; it was also the opening up of a new world of possibility. "If any man be in Christ," writes Paul, "there is a new creation (not just he is a new creature), old things are passed away; behold all things are become new."

As Weymouth adds in a footnote: "There is a new God, a new world, a new self." By consciously abiding in Christ, horizons were widened for me.

At the same time I obtained an enlarged, more accurate and more experimental view of the Third Person of the blessed Trinity. From the first I had been moved to wonder at the ineffable mystery of the Trinity which reaches its climax in the fact of the Holy Spirit. It is much that God the Father is *above* me; it is more that God the Son is *for* me; it is still more that God the Holy Spirit is *within* me. It has been well said that no one can understand the doctrine of the Incarnation of God in Christ who does not first find it incredible. But the mystery that the believer in Christ becomes an "incarnation" of God is still greater.

However, the mystery works itself out in ways most practical. And these ways I began to learn. There came a healthy corrective to a tendency to think of the Holy Spirit in terms of the external and the sensational. A revered elder friend helped me greatly when he taught me that the Holy Spirit works *in* us before He works *through* us.

Thought: Father, Son, Holy Spirit are one. So just as Jesus came to make God visible to us, so the Holy Spirit comes to make Jesus visible in us.

The Holy Spirit is Jesus made omnipresent again.

I made further advance when, through the words of another wise instructor, I was shown how the early chapters of John's Gospel set forth a progressive work of the Holy Spirit, in Chapter 8 in (1) *effecting the New Birth*, in Chapter 4 in (2) *maintaining within a constant supply of spontaneous, satisfying life* ("The water that I shall give him shall be in him a spring of water."), in Chapter 7, in (3) *causing the life to be overflowing in blessing to others.* ("Out of his inner being shall flow rivers of living water.") Again I was both challenged and encouraged.

Later I was able to relate the doctrine of the Spirit to the doctrine of Christ. I saw that He is the Baptizer into union with Christ, in identification with Whom is death, burial and resurrection. According to the Sixth of Romans, I am assured that "sin shall not have dominion over me," and that thus the Holy Spirit makes actual in me what Christ, through His Cross, has made possible. I learned that, as the Spirit of truth, He reveals Christ so that the Savior becomes a "living, bright reality"; and that, as the other Comforter, the Paraclete, the one "called alongside," He could be just as helpful to me in my life problems as Jesus was to His disciples in theirs. What riches were here!

There was yet another territory to be occupied. More slowly a third doctrine of the inner life was mastered, a doctrine comprehending and consummating the others. The Epistle to the Hebrews taught me that the Lord Jesus is the High Priest who, through His blood, has opened the Heavenly Sanctuary and entered in, not only for Himself, but also for us; therefore the soul can now enter into the Holiest of all, where God dwells; and, not only so, that the soul can be maintained in that Presence because of the present ministry of the living Priest, a ministry of continual cleansing, giving of life, and of

"We must not think of ourselves as ordinary people. We are not natural men; we are born again. God has given His Holy Spirit, and He is the spirit 'of power and of love and of a sound mind.' Therefore to those who are particularly prone to spiritual depression through timorous fear of the future, I say in the Name of God and in the words of the Apostle: 'Stir up the gift,' talk to yourself, remind yourself of who you are and what you are, and of what spirit is within you; and, having reminded yourself of the character of the Spirit, you will be able to go steadily forward, fearing nothing, living in the present, ready for the future, with one desire only, to glorify Him who gave His all for you."

D. Martyn Lloyd-Jones

intercession exercised on the authority of a new Covenant.

I am aware that these are expressions unfamiliar to the modern mind and perhaps uncongenial to it. But I testify that in this doctrine of Life in the Holiest I find the final and supreme guarantee of soul rest, as indeed, it is meant to be.

This Life in the Presence is the promised "Rest that remaineth," because here is *the supply of deficiency* necessary for soul rest. Here the High Priest ministers to us in "the power of an indissoluble life." Moreover, the ministry of life is supplemented by the ministry of sympathetic understanding and of intercession. Having been "tempted in all points like as we are," He can be "touched with the feeling of our weaknesses" and "ever liveth to make intercession for us."

And here is the *cleansing* even more necessary for soul rest. This High Priest "sprinkles the heart from an evil conscience." Here is provision for our greatest need. An experience in the life of Dr. J. H. Jowett related in his characteristic, choice language illustrates this ministry of blood in the life of the believer and here most wonderful of all is the possibility of a life lived in the Presence of a God Who Himself is restful and promises us His own rest:

"And a little while ago I had a day-dream, one of those subjective visions which sometimes visit the mind in seasons of wakeful meditation and serious thought. I was in my study in the early morning, before the day's work was begun, and I was somewhat contemplating the comparative weakness of my ministry and the many shortcomings in my personal life. And while I pondered, with closed eyes, I became aware of a Presence before Whom my spirit bowed in trembling awe. He lifted my garments, and

A similar Scripture is Romans 8:26: "The Spirit itself maketh intercession for us with groanings which cannot be uttered."

In Greek, the *with* is the dative of respect; the phrase actually means, "*with respect to* our groanings which cannot be uttered."

Were you ever at a loss for words in prayer? The Holy Spirit gathers these unspoken, un-word-able prayers and articulates them to the Father for us.

I saw that they were badly stained. He went away, and came again, and again He lifted my robes, and began to remove the stains, and I saw that He was using the ministry of blood. And then He touched my lips, and they became pure as the lips of a little child. And then He anointed mine eyes with eyesalve, and I knew He was giving sight to the blind. Then He breathed upon my brow, and my depression passed away like a morning cloud. And I wondered what next my august Companion would do, and with the eyes and ears of my spirit I watched and listened. Then He took a pen, and, putting it into my hand, He said, 'Write, for I will take of the things of Christ and show them unto thee.' And I turned to my desk and I wrote in the communion of the Holy Ghost."

Once I stood with a friendly commander on the bridge of a great liner as it ploughed its way through the Red Sea. Night was descending on the placid waters of the deep sea, which was fringed by jagged, slate-colored hills. The evening was very still. As day died heaven was, indeed, touching earth with rest.

And the ship also was quiet. No sounds came from the decks beneath. On the bridge itself, officers, intent upon their careful watch, paced without speech and with noiseless steps.

Previously, the captain, who was a Christian man, in intimate conversation in his rooms, had told our little party how grave were the responsibilities of the commander of an ocean liner. We had also learned that, at the moment, we were passing through dangerous waters.

Now on the bridge, the center of efficient control, drinking in a silence that could be felt, I said to myself many times, "The place of responsibility is the place of quiet."

"The quiet restfulness of God's unhurried presence acts as a solace to fretful and anxious hearts; moreover, in such an atmosphere the human spirit is made sensitive to the movements of the Divine Spirit, and confidence that He will not fail is engendered. It is those who thus wait, who find strength to continue waiting for His moment which assuredly will come."

Thomas Pitch

That evening Mrs. Browning's lines struck a responsive note within me:—

> And I smiled to think God's greatness
> Flowed around our incompleteness,
> Round our restlessness, His rest.

There is a rest of God. That rest, through the ministry of our High Priest, we are invited to share. Cleansed and empowered within, we can live within the Holiest of all in the Presence of God where there is rest.

Some have lived in the atmosphere of the Divine Serenity. The son of the scholarly and saintly Bishop Wescott said concerning his father, "In his later life my Father obviously lived in two worlds at once. While his feet were set in the world, his spirit was in the presence of God. Everything that came to him was met in that presence. Nothing could ever surprise him from that attitude."

That is what life in the Holiest means—and it is always restful.

The inspired writer of the Epistle to the Hebrews speaks of it as a life anchored within the veil, kept steady and secure in times of storm.

4

Adjustment to Life's Burdens

"There is no situation so chaotic that God cannot from that situation, create something that is surpassingly good. He did it at the creation. He did it at the cross. He is doing it today."

Handley C. G. Moule

4

OUR QUEST moves from the inner room of life out into the busy ways of the world. We have seen how God blesses our coming in to the sanctuary of the soul. If we are to live serenely we must also be Blessed in our going out into

> . . . the loud stunning tide
> Of human care and crime.

For this, too, there is grace—"threshold grace" as it has been called.

The practice of serenity has been perfectly exemplified in the life of Jesus. At this stage of our quest we shall be helped most effectively by observing and listening to the Man of Nazareth.

The life of Jesus was supremely reposeful. All the paths of the Master were paths of peace. That is the inescapable impression which His life makes upon us. But that is not all that has to be said. The significant thing is that, living in the manner in which He did, Jesus still preserved a spirit of calm.

Consider these striking combinations. He lived *strenuously*, yet there was always about His movements an air of leisure. The strenuousness is unmistakable. The evangelist Mark, more especially, writes of days filled with a swiftly moving succession of exacting tasks. As soon as one task was finished "immediately," "straightway," "forthwith," another

"How much greater than any of ours was Jesus' responsibility—the responsibility of saving the world! If there was ever on this earth a being who could be tempted to bustle about, to hurry everywhere, to want to see everyone in order to fulfill His task, it was Jesus Christ. But what do we see? That wondrous calm that shines forth in the Gospels. Jesus had time to speak tranquilly with a woman whom he met at the well. . . . He had time for children. He had time for those who came to Him. And His great mission, His mission for all the entire world, was fulfilled in that total giving of Himself to each person, in that calm and completely personal dialogue with each one."

Paul Tournier

45

claimed His attention. Much of His time was spent with multitudes numbering thousands. Privacy was difficult to obtain.

Yet Jesus was always leisurely. He never hurried. Even when an urgent message came from Bethany that Lazarus was dead, "He abode two days still in the same place." He required, and took, sufficient time for His plan of action to mature.

Interruptions never distracted Him. He accepted them as opportunities of a richer service. Interruptions were the occasion of some of His most gracious deeds and most revealing words.

He lived *intensely*, yet entirely without tension. The evidence of intensity is everywhere. In the presence of human need He was stirred to a compassion so deep that it affected Him physically. He was "grieved" at the hardness of men's hearts. He shed tears of sympathy as He stood with mourners. He was broken with sorrow as He contemplated the judgment of desolation about to fall on Jerusalem. He flamed with indignation as He exposed hypocrisy. Intensity indeed! Yet there is always the quick return to normal composure. If He was shaken by agony in Gethsemane, a calm dignity shows itself through all the rest of the Via Dolorosa.

He lived *dangerously*, yet always in the calm of an invincible courage. Certain Pharisees advised, "Get thee out, and depart hence: for Herod will kill thee." Anxious disciples urged Him not to go again into Judaea. "Master, the Jews, of late, sought to stone thee; and goest thou thither again?" they objected. But He was unconcerned. He told Pharisees and disciples alike that He had accepted His appointed course and, regardless of threats, He would fulfill it. When the twelfth hour of His life's day had struck, the soldiers sent to arrest Him were over-awed by the majestic calm of the Holy One, shrank back in consternation and fell to the ground.

Such was the repose of the Son of Man.

Let us pause to notice that in the light of the life of Jesus the Christian conception of rest has plainly no affinity with quietism. Various philosophies have become popular which seek to achieve serenity by repressing high ambition and by retreating from reality. Surely such philosophies are unworthy of virile men and women who seek to live positively. It is easy enough to gain peace by withdrawing from the responsibilities of life, but it is the inglorious peace of negation and of selfishness and has not the approval of Christ.

How may the restfulness of Jesus be explained? It should be remembered that, being truly human, our Lord "was tempted in all points like as we are." The "all points" included the liability to worry, to yield to the invasion of rush and of strain and of panic. But He was reposeful. He seemed to create a little island of quiet around Himself in the sea of excitement in which He habitually moved. How shall we account for this victorious calm?

In modern thought, restful living is defined in terms of harmonious adjustments. H. G. Wells attributed his unhappiness to failure in this respect. The sad record remains: "I cannot adjust myself to secure any fruitful peace. Here I am sixty-five—still seeking for peace." It is of great interest that Jesus explained His restfulness in terms of a correct adjustment.

Consider His words: "Take my yoke upon you and learn of me; for I am meek and lowly in heart: and ye shall find rest unto your souls." Keeping in mind that a yoke is the means by which the bullock is attached or adjusted to its burden, observe that Jesus said

Someone has said, "There is a sense of spaciousness about the man who walks with God."

"It is only in Him that the soul has room."

George Macdonald

> "Meek," I understand, in the original Greek meant literally the "tamed" or the "broken" (as a wild horse is broken). A wild horse is of no use to anyone, but a "meek" or "gentled" horse can give great pleasure.

> "It was our Lord's meekness and lowliness that made His great burden so light. . . . And it is out of His own experience that He speaks to us. 'Bring but a meek heart to your burden as I did,' He says to us. 'Bring but the same mind to your yoke as I brought to my yoke, and see how easy it will feel.' . . . Go to Him in any case, and whatever He sees it good to do with you and your burden, He will at any rate begin to give you another heart under it. He will begin to give you a meek and lowly heart. . . . It is not your burden that weighs you down. It is your proud, rebellious self-seeking, self-pleasing heart. . . . Had He dealt with you after your sins and rewarded you according to your iniquities, you would not have been here to find fault with the way He is leading you to pardon, peace and everlasting life."

> Alexander Whyte

these things: (1) That the way in which He was adjusted to life and its burden made for ease and rest. "My yoke is easy and my burden is light." (2) That His yoke, or adjustment to life, was meekness and lowliness. (3) That those who take His yoke upon them and learn of Him, those who, like Him, will meet life with a meek and lowly heart, will also find rest.

I urge questing souls to pay careful heed to these enlightening words. They explain the restfulness of Jesus and they point the way to rest for our own souls.

Let us trace the outworking of the spirit of meekness and lowliness in the life of Jesus and see what adjustments were effected by it. A first effect was this: in His approach to life, there was no thought whatsoever of self-interest; for meekness and lowliness are the opposites of self-seeking.

The meek and lowly Jesus was selfless. He was not merely unselfish; He was without self. He came "not to be ministered unto, but to minister." So it was throughout His whole life and, at the end, the word spoken as a sneer was sublimely true: "He saved others; Himself He cannot save." Jesus was selfless and therefore He was restful, because an adjustment to life that asks nothing for self always brings that happy result.

Let us be frank enough to accept the unpleasant truth that much of the strain of our lives can be traced to the assertion of the unsubdued self. Self-centeredness makes of life a field of tensions. We are so constituted that self-seeking inevitably brings inner disharmony. It is significant that the word "idiot" is derived from the Greek *idios*, which means "oneself."

The soul that desires serenity must take strong action. It must ruthlessly expose every apparent trace of the self-life and not let it masquerade under digni-fied disguises. It will examine its holiness for that "weasel-like thing, pride"; and its service for self-display and a maneuvering for self-advantage. It will then bravely, decisively abandon self, and every man-ifestation of it, to Christ, to be carried to His Cross for crucifixion. The surrender of self is a very care-ful, detailed, costly action, but nothing less will suf-fice. It will, moreover, bring the happy result of "a heart at leisure from itself," with new possibilities of joyous living.

Concerning this matter of dealing with an obtru-sive self, God often brings men and women to an hour of revealing which leads on to release from its tyranny. In the first flush of his preaching triumphs, the young Spurgeon was made to answer the ques-tion: "Seekest thou great things for thyself?" and to hear the injunction: "Seek them not." As he stood gazing into the waters of a stream, he told God that he would renounce the self-pretensions that threat-ened to mar his ministry.

So it was with Campbell Morgan. It was his habit to pass a short time in the loneliness of his study at the end of the day, and while sitting in contempla-tion the strange question came to him, "Are you going to be a preacher or My messenger?" Then, says Dr. Morgan, I began to look over my ministry, over the sermon I had just preached, and I discovered that subtly creeping into my life was the ambition to be a preacher. Then there came the spiritual struggle, and it was not until the grey light of dawn that the an-swer was given, "I will be Your messenger." This victory was completed when the grate was full of ashes, and the ambition to be merely a preacher flickered out as the last manuscript page of sermons was burning. From that day Dr. Morgan tried to be a

Elizabeth Strachan: "Self is spiritual B.O."

In the little village of Drumnadrocket on the shores of Loch Ness in Scotland sits a small church. Above the vestry door leading to the pulpit were written these words:

"No man can give both the impression that he himself is clever, and that Jesus is mighty to save."

Told to me by Dr. James Stewart
of Edinburgh

messenger. "If Thou wilt give me Thy words, from this day forward I will utter them as I know them," was his covenant.

The healing of such harmonizing experiences may extend beyond mind and heart to the body. During his fruitful ministry in Australia, Dr. Graham Scroggie told me of an impressive incident in his life. At one stage he had violent attacks of nausea before preaching. He was advised by an eminent medical authority to abandon the work to which he was sure God had called him. In his distress he consulted his friend Dr. Harry Guinness, who asked searchingly whether he had ever obeyed the counsel of Romans 12:1 to present our bodies a living sacrifice to God. "Yes, in a general way," answered the other. "Do it in a specific, deliberate way," suggested his saintly friend. "I went alone with God," said Dr. Scroggie, "and allowed Him to search my life. It was revealed to me that I had been cherishing a secret purpose of building up a reputation. I made confession and resolved that, henceforth, I would preach only to the glory of God. From that day the nausea ceased."

It was freely stated that, during the bombing of London, people suffering from nervous disorders found unexpected health by forgetting their own troubles in ministering to the terrible needs of victims of the air raids.

Again, the meekness and lowliness of Jesus eliminated self-sufficiency from His life. The meek and lowly Jesus was *dependent*. Though conscious of eternal Sonship He accepted a position of subordination to His Father and lived in humble dependence upon Him. He made statements like this: "I can of mine own self do nothing. The words that I speak, I speak not of myself. The Father that dwelleth in me, He doeth the works." If Jesus knew nothing of self-interest, neither did He of self-sufficiency. He was dependent.

That was an important feature of our Lord's adjustment to life. He went confidently to every task in an attitude of dependence upon God, His Father. Such an adjustment inevitably lightened life's burden for Him, for dependence is always restful. When, by love and trust, we are able to place ourselves and our affairs in the hands of one who is entirely dependable, we at once find relief from the burden of responsibility. How much more restful is dependence when it leans upon the strength and loving care of the Almighty Father. It proved to be so in the case of the Lord Jesus: So, also, it will prove to be in our case.

Let me tell you what I find when I seek to learn from Jesus how to live dependently. I find that He wants me to treat God very *simply*. He Himself did so. He talked to His Father naturally. When anything occurred that prompted Him to prayer, He at once raised His eyes towards heaven using words of the simplest kind, such as these: "Father, glorify Thy name," "Father, all things are possible to Thee," "Father, the hour is come," "Father, forgive them." I find, too, that men who have been long in the School of Jesus become simpler and simpler in their attitude towards the Heavenly Father. I find that they become as little children. Late in life Daniel Webster, as he prepared for sleep, used to offer the child's prayer beginning:

> Now I lay me down to sleep;
> I pray Thee, Lord, my soul to keep.

Samuel Chapman, intellectually and spiritually a massive and towering figure in the religious life of Australia, was called by his close friends "the Child Samuel" because, in their fellowship of prayer, he used frequently to offer in petition these words:

> Make me humble and mild.
> Just a very little child.
> Low down at Thy feet
> Blood washed and meet
> To be used, Dear Lord, by Thee.

I confess that thus to be simple towards God causes me to be very quiet.

I find, too, that the Lord Jesus teaches us to treat the Father *intimately*. It is not that He encourages us to share His own intimacy. He ruled out that possibility when He made the distinctions between "My God" and "Your God"; between "My Father" and "Your Father." But He does encourage us in our own proper degree to treat God with intimacy. Moreover, we have also the apostolic encouragement. Paul writes of those who have the "Spirit of adoption" crying to God, "Abba, Father." *Abba* is an Aramaic term of endearment only used in the close circle of a family. Advanced scholars in the School of Jesus have always dared to treat God with an intimacy quite consistent with filial fear.

Dr. Elvet Lewis has told that, in the course of a pastoral visit, a saint of his congregation said to him, "Pastor, my best times with the Lord Jesus are not when I am on my knees in formal prayer: but when I have finished praying and sit in my rocking chair chatting things over with Him." Do you not think with me that when to simplicity is added such intimacy towards God, a still deeper quiet sinks into the soul?

This, further, becomes clear to me when I seek to learn from Jesus the way of dependence. I must treat God *trustfully*. Dr. Streeter has a suggestive word about the prayers of Jesus. He says they were "not so much petitions as uttered trust." Dependence reaches fulfillment in the soul that, like Jesus, lives the life of trust. "What will you do now?" asked a friend of a mother with five children who had just been bereaved of her husband. "Now I shall prove the promises of God," answered the widow, who had already learned the way of dependence.

Deepest of all is the quiet of trust.

Being what He was, the Lord Jesus made another adjustment to life. Self-will could find no place in the life of the meek and lowly One. Jesus was not only selfless and dependent, but also *obedient*. Life for Him was a continual conscious doing of His Father's will. Everything that came to Him and every plan He made was interpreted or conceived in terms of that will. His saying "I came not to do mine own will; but the will of Him that sent me" expressed the principle that dominated His days.

That, too, is an adjustment that makes for the lightening of life's burden. Jesus found that. He said that doing the Father's will was His meat, that is, something satisfying and strengthening.

All who have lived in that way have found the same thing. Dante meant that when he wrote "In His will is our peace." Consider these things. A life lived in the will of God is a harmonious whole undistracted by differing aims and controlled by a directing mind. Moreover, such a life has a clear view of the end. It has none of the fever which rushes into activity to no purpose.

A famous scientist is said to have thrown himself into a jaunting car in Dublin and called out to the

Nothing can touch the child of God without His permission. (Read Job 1 and 2.)

"The fool hath said in his heart, There is no God" (Psalm 14:1). This goes also for those who doubt His sovereignty. Either He is sovereign or He is not. If He is not sovereign He is not God. Therefore when we become so preoccupied with and dismayed by circumstances and certain people that we doubt God's ability to handle them in His own way, and in His own time, then we too are fools.

It is this knowledge that enables us to accept the unacceptable. We can take whatever comes as from His hand, submit to it, and learn of Him all He seeks to teach us through those circumstances.

Jesus did not heal all the sick, raise all the dead, or open the eyes of every blind man during His three years on earth, yet when He reached the end of His ministry He could say, "I have finished the work which thou gavest me to do" (John 17:4).

"But Martha was cumbered about much serving" (Luke 10:40) or ". . . was distracted by waiting on many needs" (Knox).

53

coachman, "Drive fast." Away went the cab, jolting over the streets until he inquired: "Do you know where we are going?" and the driver answered, "No, but anyhow I'm driving fast."

That is a picture of the life which has no unifying aim. Those who accept the higher obedience are saved from such fruitless, wearying living. Moreover, they know the joy of the determined allegiance of the Psalmist's song, "My heart is fixed, O God, my heart is fixed. I will sing and give thanks." To live in the will of God is also to have a proper sense of dignity. Much of our trouble comes from a feeling that much of our work does not seem worthwhile. But if God appoints it, what importance is attached to it! Browning has a line:

All service ranks the same with God.

After a transforming spiritual experience, Hudson Taylor wrote these typical lines to his mother: "I am more happy in the Lord than I have ever been, and enjoy more leisure of soul, casting more fully every burden on Him Who, alone, is able to bear all. To be content with God's will and way is rest. Things may not be, in many respects, as I would wish them; but if God permits them to be so or so orders them, I may be well content. Mine is to obey, His to direct."

5

Leaving It All Quietly to God

"Not always talking to Him or about Him, but waiting before Him; till the stream runs clear; till the cream rises to the top; till the mists part, and the soul regains its equilibrium."

F. B. Meyer

5

IN THE Sixty-Second Psalm occur the words which sink softly into the heart when strain and stress threaten to disturb its poise. Moffatt renders it: "Leave it all quietly to God, my soul." The Psalmist's counsel has been of such help to me in my quest for serenity that I want to share it with fellow seekers. Let the Psalmist guide us now in the practice of peace.

Leave it all quietly to God, my soul. Obviously, there is possible danger in an exhortation like that. To wait "only on God," as the authorized version has it, might encourage a quiet which is only quiescence, a quiet which sits with folded hands in supine ease. The Psalmist had no such intention. There is something of passivity in His attitude to God, but it is entirely consistent with, and indeed demands, proper human activity.

General Booth, strong man of action as he was, loved to tell of a little girl who was distressed that her small brother trapped birds. One night she added a petition to her usual bedtime prayer. "And please, dear Lord, don't let Willie catch the nice little birds." Then, rising to her feet, she said happily to her mother: "He won't be able to catch them now, Mummie." "You have great faith," answered Mother. "But he can't," said the child, "I smashed all his traps." Surely God approved of her adding such works to prayer.

For the One Who Is Tired

"Dear heart, God does not say
    today, 'Be Strong!'
He knows your strength is
    spent, He knows how long
The road has been, how weary
    you have grown;
For He who walked the earthly
    roads alone,
Each bogging lowland and each
    long, steep hill,
Can understand, and so He
    says, 'Be Still
And know that I am God.' The
    hour is late
And you must rest awhile, and
    you must wait
Until life's empty reservoirs fill
    up
As slow rain fills an empty,
    upturned cup.
Hold up your cup, dear child,
    for God to fill.
He only asks today that you be
    still."

         Grace Noll Crowell

57

Nevertheless, the Psalmist's faith is valid. It is an unquestionable fact that, God and man being what they are, we are shut up to God. For God is God and not man. He is the "I am," the "I am that I am," which is the "style not only of permanence, but of permanence self-contained. To the proud, godless world He says, 'resistance to my will can only show forth all its power. I sit upon the throne not only supreme, but independent, not only victorious, but unassailable: self-contained, self-poised, and self-sufficing.'"

This God has Sovereign Will which overrides or takes up into itself all lesser wills. That Will is finally irresistible. As Moody used to say, a man cannot really break the law of God: it will sooner or later break him. Also, that will is unchangeable. God may adapt Himself to man's waywardness just as a master chess player adapts his moves to his opponent's game; but God never alters His purposes. "I am the Lord; I change not."

And man is man; not God. A Thomas Henley may cry: "I am the master of my fate. I am the captain of my soul," but he convinces very few. A Swinburne may exclaim, in an excess of humanistic enthusiasm: "Glory to man in the highest," but most will write him down as an obscurantist and foolish, for they know that all too often man descends to the lowest. Man is man and not God and, in his heart, knows that he is shut up to God. "Gentlemen," said Lincoln one day to his generals, "I have often been driven to my knees by an overwhelming conviction that I had nowhere else to go."

Understanding all that, let us make the widest possible use of the Psalmist's words. Consider first that we may leave *our sin* quietly to God. Because Jesus died for our sins, that is a glad possibility.

But let us be sure to do it. Even some of the greatest saints do not seem to have known full evangelical peace. In this, humbly we must insist, they have fallen short of the New Testament ideal, which is restful enjoyment of the fruits of Divine pardon.

One of my own revered spiritual masters, Alexander Whyte of Free St. George's, Edinburgh, known as the last of the Puritans, was deficient in this respect. His friend, Marcus Dodds, said how much Whyte mourned over the evil of his heart. Moreover, the deficiency revealed itself in his preaching. Once he chose as his text St. Paul's famous words, "where sin abounded, grace did much more abound." He informed his hearers that he had been reading Martin Luther.

"Let us summon the spirit of Luther to our midst to hear what he has to say on this verse," he declared to his people. Opening the door which led to the pulpit, he beckoned the imaginary reformer to stand beside him. "Martin Luther," said Whyte solemnly, "what am I to say to this people on this text?"

"What does it say? 'Grace did abound.' Do you know anything, then, about grace, Alexander Whyte?"

"Not very much," was the slow reply.

"Stand aside and let me speak to this people about grace," and forthwith Whyte began to read extracts from Luther's works on grace. Having completed these, he turned to the imaginary figure and asked:

"What else should be said on this text, Martin Luther?"

"What more does the text say? 'Where sin abounded.' Do you know anything about sin, Alexander Whyte?"

"Sin," replied the minister in his thunderous voice. "Sin! Martin Luther, you may take your leave.

"We must be willing to forgive ourselves the sins which God has forgiven us."

Sin! I know all about sin and will speak to this people on that." And forthwith, Whyte spoke on the blackness of the human heart, as only he could.

One asks seriously whether the scriptural balance was preserved in such an utterance—"Where sin abounded, grace did much more abound," wrote Paul. Should not, therefore, the emphasis, both in life and preaching, be rather upon grace and the peace in which it so happily issues?

Contained in the words of the Twenty-Third Psalm, "Thou preparest a table before me in the presence of mine enemies," is a beautiful picture of the spiritual rest and enjoyment which God wants us to have. They represent the speaker as a criminal fugitive who is being pursued by the avengers of blood. They are hot upon his trail when he reaches a shepherd's tent. By Eastern law, such a fugitive would not only be protected with all the resources of the person to whose mercy he appeals, but he would also be given the best hospitality which the encampment could offer.

Here then is the fugitive being regaled at the sheik's table while the pursuers on the other side of the threshold glare at him in impotent rage. In the Psalmist's thought, the pursuers are the sins which have come from the evil past of a man who flees to God for mercy. In His keeping he is entirely safe from the blood-guiltiness of sin. For him who finds refuge in a forgiving God, there is not pursuing vengeance, but a table prepared by God's bounty.

Festal living is still more typical of the New Testament. "Christ our passover is sacrificed for us: therefore let us keep festival," wrote Paul. The atmosphere of the New Testament is one of radiant happiness begotten of an experience of sins forgiven, covered by the Savior's blood and then left quietly to God.

Perhaps each man, both Whyte and Morling, were writing from the perspective of their own spiritual pilgrimage.

Illustration: A minister in the north of England who, oppressed by guilt, had a breakdown, was advised by a wise doctor to concentrate on biblical passages expressing love, mercy, and forgiveness, *temporarily* putting aside the ones on condemnation and judgment. The minister followed the doctor's advice, and he was wonderfully restored.

"No faith can have vitality or hope which does not hold that we are somehow the better for our failures and our falls, however much they may have devastated our life and influence, with whatever shame and self-reproach they may have wasted our days."

From Benson's *Life of Ruskin*

Associated with our sin is the specter of the "might have been." A careless action, an error of judgment, even a foolish word can change the course of a life and involve us in bitter regrets and self-chiding for the rest of our days. Thus it was with Lord Curzon, whose last years were clouded by dark regrets that he had accepted appointment as Viceroy of India. During his term of office his wife had died and, for the rest of his days, the distinguished statesman rebuked himself for not having discerned that the climate would undermine her health. Far better is it to leave all such untoward things quietly to God. As God of nature, our Heavenly Father wondrously renews the face of bushland after it has been seared by fire. As God of our lives He will put forth similar recuperative powers and restore to us the years. We can well afford also to leave the specter of the "might have been" quietly to Him.

The Psalmist's counsel has relevance not only to the sense of sin, but also to *perplexity*. I have in mind particularly the perplexity which arises out of dark experiences. Few travelers on life's highway escape the challenge to faith that comes to them from some stark happening.

At such an hour of crisis we can do one of three things. We can follow the way of stoicism, which hurls defiance at fate "or whatever gods there be" and cries, "My head is bloody but unbowed." But not thus is the "deep thunder" of our "want and woe" silenced.

Or, as we may allow to happen far too often, we may yield place to doubt. Let it be said quite frankly that in such a reaction there is nothing but weakness and folly. It means either crumpling up or becoming cynical; and the strong are ashamed to crumple up, whilst the wise avoid cynicism as they do all nasty things.

"I am haunted by a feeling of guilt," Pat said to me two weeks after Gregg killed himself. "I keep wondering if I did everything I could."

"Sometimes something happens which recalls great pain. You are not able to find pleasure in that thing. The word comes, LET GO DISPLEASURE. Displeasure is not always wrath; it is not unkindness or fretting. It is just something that is not pleasure but pain, and so can depress the heart. Let it go. Do not hold onto it. Let it slip out of mind. Turn to something that does give pleasure and fasten your heart to that. 'Commit thy way (and the way of those thou lovest) unto the Lord and put thy trust in Him. . . . Hold thee still in the Lord, and abide patiently upon Him. . . . let go displeasure . . . and thou shalt be refreshed in the multitude of peace.' (Psalm 37:5, 7, 8, 11 PB)"

Amy Carmichael

"The years that the locust hath eaten" (Joel 2:25).

61

The difficulty created by the "giant agony of the world" has engaged the attention of the greatest minds of the ages, yet no complete answer of an intellectual kind has ever been given. But if intellectual theory does not provide an answer, the experience of life does; and, since life is larger than logic, the practical answer is of greater value. An answer that satisfies the heart is worth more than one that does no more than inform and convince the mind. The fact is that we find the solution to life's problems only when the problems vanish.

God has not given us the full explanation of the presence of evil in the world. We understand a good deal when we realize that this world in which there is so much pain is a "vale of soul making," but that only takes us part of the way towards an explanation.

But, we repeat, there is a solution that comes out of life. It is this: that when faith bravely, patiently, trustingly faces its personal problem, it finds that the problem disappears in an experience of God which dispels all doubts and resentments.

A fine story told of a professor of Harvard University effectively illustrates this higher mode of facing perplexity. The professor sought an interview with Phillips Brooks upon a certain problem. He spent a radiant hour with the great preacher and came out a changed man whose life was transfigured. But presently it dawned upon him that during the interview he had quite forgotten to ask Phillips Brookes about his problem! He says, however, "I did not care; I had found out that what I needed was not the solution of a special problem, but the contagion of a triumphant spirit."

If the answer to the enigmas of life is to be found in an attitude rather than in an inquiry, what is that attitude?

Some problems cannot vanish. Illustration: My dear friend Nancy Bates. For nearly forty years she has been confined to a wheelchair, from which she has a remarkable ministry.

This I question. Some problems have no solution.

Illustration: the paraplegic, the quadriplegic, families of suicide, and other hideous, unsolvable problems. Perhaps Amy Carmichael's beautiful line, "In acceptance lieth peace," fits in here.

As I read the stories of triumphant sufferers, I find that, by faith, they do three things that enable them to rise superior to their pain. In faith they accept their trial. They do not exhaust their energies in futile questionings, nor do they become resentful. They take, instead, an attitude of positive acceptance. It is the positiveness that makes the difference. They go even beyond resignation in regarding their trouble as being in some way, they know not how, within the scope of God's plan and, as such, something to be accepted, not merely endured.

In that brave attitude of faith the noble Dr. Edward Wilson sank into his last sleep amid the snows of Antarctica. Before he died, he wrote to his wife words which are a sublime expression of the faith which accepts positively its trial as from the hand of God.

We read with reverence these two extracts from his last letters: "I shall simply fall and go to sleep in the snow, and I have your little books with me in my breast pocket. . . . Don't be unhappy—all is for the best. We are playing a good part in a great scheme arranged by God himself, and all is well. . . ."

"I leave this life in absolute faith and happy belief that if God wishes you to wait long without me it will be to some good purpose. All is for the best to those that love God, and oh, my Ory, we have both loved Him with all our lives. All is well. . . ."

I find, too, that triumphant sufferers find relief from their pain in making their experience minister to others. They convert their own loss into gain. The positiveness of their faith leads on to creativeness.

Josephine Butler did that. Returning home one evening with her husband she was greeted by their little daughter who, in her excitement, leaned too far over the stair rail, fell to the hallway beneath and lay

—Though I don't think it true that faith never asks "Why?" Even our Lord once asked "Why?" At times faith, numb in the face of hideous, senseless tragedy may well cry, "Why?" But if God chooses to remain silent, faith is content.

"The awful patient ways of God"

J. B. Phillips

Second Corinthians 6:4: "In all things approving ourselves . . . in much patience, in afflictions, in necessities, in distresses."

Patience in Greek means literally *endurance*. It is more than patient submissiveness; there is a note of triumph. It is the ability to bear things in such a triumphant way that it transfigures them. It enables a man to pass the breaking point and not to break, and always to greet the unseen with a cheer.

Example: Joni Earickson Tada, who became a quadriplegic as the result of a diving accident, has been given a unique ministry to handicapped people all over the world. She edits a paper, *We Have Wheels*, lectures, sings, paints (beautifully, with a brush held between her teeth), and on and on. . . . She's incredible!

63

dying at their feet. After the first shock of her grief had passed, Mrs. Butler, with her husband's blessing, opened her home to shelter fallen girls. As she put it, "I have now no daughter of my own, so I shall be a mother to any girl who needs me." And, in saving others, she saved herself.

Faith accepts positively; acts creatively; then, as its crowning expression, acquiesces restfully. Having been active, it becomes passive and leaves its problem quietly to God.

I have found that the noblest sufferers have been able to do this the more readily when it has been borne home to their hearts that God has also suffered and still suffers. Dr. Carnegie Simpson has made this strong declaration. "If God is not One who stands apart from human suffering, even though holding the explanation of it in His hand, but One who comes into it and shares it, that is a thought of God upon which faith could stand in any anguish. That character in God, that passion in God, would be faith's deliverance."

God *is* such a God. If men suffer, so, in Christ, did He suffer. If men suffer because of the wrongdoing of others, so did He. Once they have seen that, men and women of faith have been able to leave their perplexity quietly to God. Such men and women understand what the Lord Jesus meant when He said: "In that day ye shall ask me no questions."*

I suggest one other application of the Psalmist's admonition. It has relevance also to the *foreboding* that so often robs life of its sunshine. Foreboding, which is a secret fear of the future, may relate to our personal affairs, to our spiritual development, and to our life service. In respect to the first, foreboding has

*John 16:23, Moffatt.

> Dan Piatt (who lost three members of his family in one car accident) said after the tragedy: "I told God that I wanted to learn everything He had to teach me through this experience."

> "What I do thou knowest not now; but thou shalt know hereafter" (John 13:7). "Heaven is the place where questions and answers become one."
>
> Eli Wiesel

no place in the life that has learned to leave all quietly to God.

Paul speaks of a peace of God that "passes understanding," by which he means a peace that extends beyond the point of human "minding" or planning. Very properly we make provision for the future, financial and otherwise, but we cannot provide against every contingency and, in any case, our "minding" is necessarily confined to time. God's "minding" for us, however, foresees everything and reaches into eternity, so that for those who live in the world of God there are no uncertainties.

We can live very restfully when we have left the future quietly to the Father Who knows all that will come to us and has already provided for it. Let us, however, be sure that we do this with real quietness. Some of us can make a great burden of casting our burdens on the Lord.

Likewise is there rest for the soul that, giving all proper attention to spiritual culture, leaves its growth in the care of the Father. How well I remember the encouragement that came to me at a time of depression when an older friend who was "Far Ben" (as the Scotch describe the mature saint) reminded me of Paul's reassuring word—"He that hath begun a good work in you will perform it until the day of Christ."

The Lord Jesus spoke of what one has called the "law of the lily," which God arrays even though it neither toils nor spins. All that the flower does to cultivate its beauty is to respond to the divine forces amidst which it is set. So also does God clothe with glory the life that quietly leaves its development to Him. There must always be a hungering and thirsting after righteousness, but let us always remember the "law of the lily."

Above my desk hangs a handpainted, framed

> "Fear not the future
> God is already there."

God's grace is not only sufficient —it is inexhaustible. I remember hearing a story about a little fish who said, "I am so thirsty but I must not drink too much. The ocean might run dry"—or the little mouse in the granaries of Egypt who said, "I am so hungry. But I must not eat too much. The grain might not last."

Whatever the need—"He giveth more grace" (James 4:6).

Now need there be no foreboding about the result of life service. The servant of Christ who realizes that not only does he work for God, but also with Him, can well afford to leave that also quietly to God.

I have often found encouragement in the story of the Italian painter who, in old age, had lost something of his former skill. One evening he sat dejectedly before a painting which he had just completed, conscious that he had not been able to impart the touch which used to cause his canvases to glow with life. As he went off to bed he was heard to say sadly, "I have failed, I have failed." Later his son, who was also an artist, came into the studio to examine his father's work. He too was aware of deficiency. Then, taking palette and brush, he worked on into the night, until under his younger hand the picture fulfilled the father's vision. In the morning, not knowing what had been done, the older man went into the studio and stood in delight before the transformed picture: "Why," he exclaimed, "I have wrought better than I knew."

With reverent caution, may we not regard the story as a parable? When life's day is done will parents, teachers, and all who have faithfully worked with God discover that they have wrought better than they knew? Did not the Psalmist encourage us to think so when he wrote, "Thou wilt perfect that which concerneth me?"

Leave it all quietly to God, my soul. We shall have advanced a long way in the quest for serenity when we can intelligently and strongly speak thus to ourselves.

Leave quietly to God also:

My mistakes.
The sins and shortcomings of others.
The mistakes of others.
That which is none of my business.
Politics and world affairs.
That which I cannot get done.
And that which I cannot get undone.
The un-understandable.
That for which I am not remotely responsible.

"God grant me the serenity to accept the things I cannot change, the courage to change the things I can, and the wisdom to know the difference."

6

Living Restfully with God

"Before the winds that blow do
    cease,
  Teach me to dwell within Thy
    calm;
Before the pain has passed in
    peace,
  Give me, my God, to sing a
    psalm;
Let me not lose the chance to
    prove
The fullness of enabling love.
  O Love of God, do this for me;
  Maintain a constant victory."

Amy Carmichael
Edges of His Ways, p. 37

6

OUR QUEST has made it clear that, in the attainment of serenity, it is our life in God that matters most. We cannot hope to live restfully unless we live restfully with God. Equally plain is it that just here lies the explanation of our failure.

Dr. J. H. Jowett insisted that it was only a restful church that could successfully oppose the general restlessness, the heated and consuming haste of the world, but was compelled to confess that "the care-lines and the wrinkles of worry and anxiety and uncertainty and a general air of restlessness seem to me almost as prevalent upon the countenance of the Church as upon the face of the world." He traced the cause to the undue emphasis in spiritual culture upon the "great, hot, dry, words: strive, fight, wrestle, oppose, work, war, do, endeavour" and the neglect of "those gracious energizing words, lying there with the soft dews upon them: grace, rest, quietness, assurance." Jowett's assessment of the situation raises into greater urgency the questions: How shall we live restfully with God?

I propose to discuss that question against the background of the Quakers' technique. Of all Christian groups, the Quakers have most directly sought to live in the "chamber called peace." And not without success. Charles Lamb said that he had been in a Quaker meeting over which "the Dove seemed almost visibly brooding." A modern writer says that

"The yield of our life does not depend so much on the number of things that we do, but more on the quality of self-giving that we put to each thing. In order to add this quality, we must depart from this atmosphere of the modern world which is completely obsessed with activism, even in the church: do, do, do always more. Let us rather, once again, become inspired and tranquil men."

Paul Tournier

LIVING RESTFULLY
WITH GOD

"the very peace of God steeps their spirits and chastens and refines their manners, gives softness to their speech and appears to impart leisureliness even to the very activities of their bodies."

I am concerned primarily with the technique, not with the doctrine of the Quakers. There has been among them considerable variety of belief which they have not found to be inconsistent with the central doctrine of the Inner Light. Warm evangelicals have been numbered among them. Their technique, therefore, is applicable within the framework of the full evangelical faith.

Three words stand out in the vocabulary of Quaker culture: inwardness, passiveness, stillness. It is in the cultivation of these attitudes that they have found it possible to live restfully with God.

There is the attitude of *inwardness*. Quakers make much of first-hand experience, of immediacy, and much less of "knowledge—about." A precursor of George Fox, their real founder, asks in a fine passage "in what Blessedness lieth?" He answers that it is not in anything whatever *outside us*—"Not in works nor wonders that God hath wrought, or ever shall work so far as these things exist or are done outside. These things can make me blessed only in so far as they exist or are done and loved, known, tasted, and felt *within* me."

It was after George Fox had been brought to despair by outward forms of religion that he learned "there was an Anointing *within* man to teach him and that the Lord would teach His people Himself." He tells of a transforming experience: "When all my hope in them (Church leaders) and in all men was gone, so that I had nothing *outwardly* to help me, nor could tell what to do, then, O then I heard a voice which said, 'there is One, even Christ Jesus,

"The true meaning of meditation is to deepen our intimacy with God; it is to learn to live in constant communion with Jesus Christ, to share everything with Him. To seek our path each day with Him is above all to learn to know Him and to make Him really a party to our life."

Paul Tournier

that can speak to thy condition'; and, when I heard it, my heart did leap for joy."

This fact of inwardness determines the method of Quakers which may be seen best in the journal of John Woolman, perhaps their greatest saint. This sweet apostle of love uses such expressions as these: "My mind was frequently covered with inward prayer"; "The case being new and unexpected, I made no answer suddenly, but at a time silent, my mind being inward"; "In these opportunities my mind, through the mercies of the Lord, was kept low in an inward waiting for His help."

I offer some comments on this way of inwardness. It is not unnecessary to urge some caution in respect to the Quaker thought of God. We must balance the fact of the God Who is within by that of the God Who is without and above. As one of the best Quaker thinkers has said: "It is the Beyond who is within." To say with Behmen that "the kingdom of heaven, the throne of grace, the Son of God, the Holy Ghost, are all within thee" is not to state the whole truth about God. Nor must we assume that, in the full Christian sense, God dwells in man as he is naturally constituted. The New Testament anointing presupposes a spiritual new birth.

Another cautionary word may be added. The inward look may easily be directed towards oneself instead of towards the Divine Indweller. "How is your soul, David?" asked a former acquaintance of Livingstone on his return from Africa. "My soul, my soul!" answered that great man of God, in mild surprise. "I had almost forgotten that I had a soul." But he had not forgotten Christ and souls for whom Christ died. "For every one look at yourself take ten looks at Jesus Christ," advised Robert Murray McCheyne.

More (deeper) than introspection—this looking to the Christ dwelling within us.

"I would not look within;
Then would I feel most lost.
Myself hath nought
On which to stay my trust:
Nothing but failures, weak
    endeavors
Crumbling into dust;
I must look up by faith
To Jesus, Lord—
For there is faith and hope
    and love
And grace—with every need
    supplied."

Author Unknown

However, having made these safeguards, let us deliberately practice the way of inwardness, for it is the way of spiritual reality. In the temple within, created by the Holy Spirit in regeneration, we find in holy immediacy the Indwelling God. May I ask whether you, who have joined me in this quest, know anything of God *at first hand*; whether you know the difference between saying formal words and phrases in prayer and coming into vital communion with God; whether you have had the poet's experience:

For a moment on the soul
Falls the rest that maketh whole,
Falls the endless peace.

If not, hear the Savior's promise as though you had never heard it before. He, the Holy Spirit, the Other Comforter, the Higher Mode in which Christ Himself is present, "shall be with you and shall be *within* you!" You have not known spiritual reality because you have not used the way of inwardness.

It appears to me that the way of inwardness implies three things. There must first of all be an opening of the understanding to comprehend the mystery of God's Indwelling. Seeing that your quest must end in failure unless there is clear thinking and sincere response at this point, may I urge that, now and often, you kneel and offer a prayer such as this: "Most Holy God, in adoring wonder I bow before Thee in the presence of this wondrous mystery of grace: my spirit, soul and body Thy temple. In deep silence and worship I accept the blessed revelation, that in me, too, there is a Holiest of all, and that there Thy hidden Glory has its abode. O my God, forgive me that I have so little known it. I do now tremblingly accept the blessed truth: God the Spirit, the Holy Spirit, who is God Almighty, dwells in me."*

The best of the Quakers speak also of "orientation around the Divine Center within." Professor Thomas R. Kelly, whose *Testament of Devotion* has greatly enriched me, says that the practice of inward orientation is the heart of religion. He defines it mainly in terms of inward surrender. Meister Eckhart is quoted: "There are plenty to follow our Lord half-way, but not the other half. They will give up possessions, friends, and honors, but it touches them too closely to disown themselves."

He pleads for the obedience of the other half, and speaks suggestively of "fugitive islands of secret reservations," as also of a life which is "as sensitive as a shadow, selfless as a shadow, obedient as a shadow." He wants Christians to fling themselves into the cause of Christ with all the passion of dedicated lives instead of having a mild and mediocre religion. He quotes William James as saying that, in some, religion exists as a dull habit, in others as an acute fever, and refuses to believe that religion as a dull habit is that for which Christ lived and died.

Orientation of life round the center is certainly a very searching affair. Even that is not all. Detachment must be supplemented by attachment to that Center of love. What choice words are these from our Professor: "Let me talk very intimately and very earnestly with you about Him who is dearer than life. Do you really want to live your lives, every moment of your lives, in His Presence? Do you long for Him, crave Him? Do you love His Presence? Does every drop of blood in your body love Him? Does every breath you draw breathe a prayer,

*From Andrew Murray's *The Spirit of Christ*.

Submit to God (Genesis 16:9, Luke 2:51, James 4:6–8a)

Delight in Him (Psalm 37:4)

Learn His lessons (Psalm 25:4–5, Psalm 27:11, Matthew 11:29)—Be God's eager pupil!

Worship Him when you cannot understand (Job 1:20, 1 Samuel 1:28, 2 Samuel 15:32, 12:20).

Shift goals from personal happiness to His glory (John 11:24–28). "Man's chief end is" not personal happiness, but "to glorify God and to enjoy Him forever."

73

The Great Spirit scooped up the tiny chipmunk and held him cupped in his hand. "Let me down! Let me down!" cried the little chipmunk. "You are interrupting me!"

"Why?" asked the Great Spirit, "What are you in such a great hurry about? Stay in my hand."

"Let me down! Let me down! I must mop up the flood. See, I dip my tail in it and wring it out and dip it again and wring it out. Hurry and put me down."

Looking down, the Great Spirit saw the little chipmunk's mate stranded on a tiny isle surrounded by water from a sudden rainstorm and smiled tenderly at the brave little chipmunk dipping his tail in and wringing it out, dipping his tail in and wringing it out.

"Here," he said, scooping him up again, "let me help you." And the Great Spirit blew with his breath and the waters disappeared.

Then the Great Spirit lovingly stroked the little chipmunk before he set him down. And the stroking made stripes down the little chipmunk's back. And he never forgot.

Based on an Indian legend told me by Helen Morken at Arrowhead Springs August 22, 1965

a praise to Him? Do you sing and dance within yourselves, as you glory in His love? Have you set yourselves to be His, and only His, walking every moment in holy obedience?"

Finally the way of inwardness implies a constant returning to the Center. In other words, it means consulting the Holy Spirit about everything we do.

We are now well on the way to living restfully with God. A supplementary attitude is that of *passiveness*. The Quaker teaching is that, because God is ever coming to us, we need not anxiously strive to realize His Presence, but in love and desire, wait for Him to disclose Himself.

Here are typical expressions: "The accent will be laid upon God, God the initiator, God the aggressor, God the striver into life." "There come times when the Presence steals upon us, not the product of agonized effort." "The creative God comes into our souls. An increment of infinity is about us. The Hound of Heaven is on our track, the God of Love is wooing us to His holy life."

All this is in line with Pascal's great word: "We should not seek if we were not already found." Patient experimenting on the basis of this fact will revolutionize devotion. We cannot really pray unless we are consciously in God's Presence. Perhaps you have found it difficult to gain this sense of God. I suggest that you adopt this method. Remembering that God is ever coming to His children, do not strain to draw God out of a seemingly silent heaven. Instead, simply let your heart go out towards Him and wait confidently for Him to come to you. Don't try to find God. *Let yourself be found of Him.*

What shall we say to these things? For myself I accept the rebuke that religious busyness, "overactivism," is a sign that one is still in spiritual adolescence. Maturity is marked by the repose in which lieth power. Therefore, I believe that, increasingly, I should endeavor to be silent unto God and should take time for that blessed culture. Already I have found that, when calm is upon the spirit, one is drawn out more readily in adoration.

It is in the silence that the Father's care, the Savior's cleansing, and the Comforter's strengthening are experienced, and worship becomes almost inevitable.

Further, I believe that, as I learn more effectively the way of stillness, I shall be able the better to use prayer.

> I am listening, Lord, to Thee;
> What hast Thou to say to me?

Inwardness: Passiveness: Stillness. Can we not imagine Francis of Assisi calling them his three sweet sisters gently guiding him into restful living with God?

"It is good that a man should both hope and quietly wait for the salvation of the Lord" (Lamentations 3:26).

7

Initiation into a Secret

"Am I not enough, Mine own?
Enough Mine own, for thee?"

*   *   *

"All thou shalt find at last
Only in Me.
Am I not enough, Mine own?
I forever and alone,
I needing Thee."

Gerhardt Tersteegen

7

WE TURN back from technique to basic principle. The one all-comprehensive fact of the New Testament is Jesus Christ. The quest which began with Christ must also end with Christ.

The Apostle Paul shall be both our teacher and our example in respect to this. Our interest is awakened by words which Paul wrote quite late in his splendid life. "I have learned," declared Paul to the Church at Philippi, "in whatsoever state I am, therewith to be content."

A dear friend, wasted by great and long suffering, commented smilingly as I read that passage to him, "You see, even Paul had to learn contentment." He was quite right. The ardent, sensitive, energetic, adventurous, combative Paul was not restful by nature. He found it just as difficult as we do, perhaps even more difficult, to live serenely. Yet, in all honesty he made the claim to have achieved a contented spirit even though he wrote from prison with a shackle on his wrist and the headsman's axe hanging by a thread over his neck. Other notable exiles of the ancient world, Cicero, Ovid and Paul's contemporary, Seneca, wrote to their friends letters full of bitter complaining and frantic appeal. In vivid contrast, Paul, in a case far worse than theirs, sent to Philippi an epistle bathed in sunshine not for the purpose of getting help but of giving it.

"My contentment lieth in knowing that all is well between us."

The deep explanation of Paul's contentment is given in an interesting passage. In referring to his peace, he spoke of being initiated into a secret. "In everything and in all things," he wrote, "I have been let into the secret of being fed full and of being hungry, of running over and of coming short."

That secret was the open secret to which we have referred. Myers expresses it perfectly in the opening lines of his poem, St. Paul:

Christ! I am Christ's! and let the name suffice you.
Ay, for me, too, He greatly hath sufficed.

Paul's secret was Jesus Christ appropriated, obeyed, used, enjoyed.

The glowing personal testimony contained in this letter reveals three outworkings of the initiation which Paul had received.

He was expressing such "joy and peace in believing" because in Jesus Christ he possessed the Rest of Heart Satisfaction, the Rest of Inner Harmony, and the Rest of Adequate Resources. Let us consider these aspects of Paul's open secret.

It has been said that the most complete picture of happiness that ever was or can be drawn is that given in the Shepherd Psalm: "He maketh me to lie down in green pastures; He leadeth me beside the still waters." By a true instinct the devout have applied the words to the experience of those who feed their souls on the truth of Christ. The green pastures are the doctrines of grace, sweet and full for the longing soul. The lying down is the supreme contentment of those who find rest in the promises of Christ. The still waters are the times of seclusion when we go alone with God.

Only the satisfied soul enjoys contentment. A browsing sheep does not lie down until it has had enough. It is quite evident that, at this time, Paul was living in such contentment because his heart was constantly feeding on Christ and finding in Him such satisfaction that no trace of unrest remained.

In these prison epistles we often meet with the word *riches*, whether it be the "unsearchable riches of Christ," the "riches of grace," or the "riches of glory." Paul had a sense of opulence even though he suffered want in his prison.

One is reminded of a poor member of James Smeatham's class meeting who "sold a bit of tea . . . and staggered along in June days with a tendency to hernia and prayed as if he had a fortune of ten thousand a year, and were the best-off man in the world." Again Paul's heart satisfaction is apparent in the conscious joyousness which sings through his pages. "I rejoice in the Lord greatly. . . . I pray and rejoice with you all," he writes. Christ does that for very many. "He rings every bell in my tower," said a brilliant young Englishman in speaking of the happiness which Christ brought him.

Still more clearly is the apostle's inner contentment revealed of his inability to determine whether life or death were the higher good. For to me, to live is Christ; and to die is gain . . . which I shall choose, I do not know. I am in a strait betwixt two, "having a desire to depart and be with Christ which is far better."

For many life and death are two evils between which it is difficult to choose. For Paul they were two great boons, each so blessed that Paul was embarrassed about choosing between them. Life, for him, was Christ. Death was more Christ. On the

> "The lonely, weary road he trod.
> 'Enter into my joy,' said God.
> The sad ascetic shook his head,
> 'I've lost all taste for joy,' he
>   said."
>
> Quoted by Amy Carmichael

> "It would be scarcely necessary to explain doctrine if our life were radiant enough."
>
> Pope John to Giacomo Menzu

81

whole, preference lay with departure, but he desired to live on in order to serve others. How healthy and radiant was the outlook of such a man!

That was one of the outworkings of Paul's secret. Christ meant for him *the rest of heart satisfaction* and, distressing as his circumstances were, he was well content.

Others beside Paul have found that Christ gives a heart satisfaction which transforms the face of life. Dr. C. H. Morrison tells a beautiful story of a friend who used to collect charities in a Scottish village. One of the cottages she had to visit was that of a pious and reverent old woman. Betty was in very straitened circumstances, but she would have been insulted if the collector had passed the door. One day when the girl called, Betty was sitting at tea. She rose to get her widow's mite out of the chest and threw her apron hastily over the tea-table. Whereupon, in girlish curiosity the friend peeped under and saw the hidden cup was filled with water! "Why, Betty," she cried in astonishment, "it isn't tea you've got here; it's water." "Ay, my dear, it's just water. *But He makes it taste like wine!*" When Christ is in the heart, the winter of discontent gives place to a glorious experience of springtide.

There was another way in which Paul's secret operated. In Christ he found *the rest of inner harmony.*

The unrest and unhappiness of many a life may be traced to the conflict of two purposes, each of which strives for the mastery. We are so constituted that for successful living we must be dominated by one ideal, one purpose, one passion. Otherwise we waste our strength in the restlessness of inner discord.

The greatest enemy of peace may well be within our own bisected personality.

"'But [Jesus], passing through the midst of them, went his way' (Luke 4:30).

"Our new month will bring us joys, for the Lord of joy is with us; it will also bring us sorrows, for sorrows are part of life. It may bring things which would 'throw us down' (Luke 4:9) if they could. But they need not ever do that, for it is possible for us to do just what our Master did when, passing through the midst of them, He went His way.

"As by His grace we go on in quietness, we shall find those words we knew so well come true: 'My presence shall go with thee, and I will give thee rest' (Exodus 33:14)."

Amy Carmichael

Paul had no inner schisms, because his whole being was under the single sway of Jesus Christ, Who was Paul's absolute Lord exercising a totalitarian control. In respect to his Master, Paul thought about himself only as a bond-slave. Christ was Paul's shining ideal of character and of service. On the pursuit of that ideal all his energies were bent. "This one thing I do," he said, and Christ was Paul's absorbing love. There could be no rival loves. His devoted heart could only be bent on the great paradox "to know the love of Christ which passeth knowledge."

What integrating forces are these which Christ set in operation in Paul's life! Here is another explanation of his peace. There were no conflicts in his inmost self. Having an end he made all things serve and, in consequence, lived rhythmically.

Perhaps we appreciate the Lord Jesus more as the Satisfier than as the Unifier. But, as Unifier, He is just as necessary to our peace as He is as Satisfier. I heard an outstanding Christian described by a medical man as a "neurotic gone right." Many of us are in that category. We have mental health only because Christ is not only Lover but also Lord of our lives, controlling the troubled kingdom that each of us has within himself. How thankful we should be that, with Christ taking up all the eddying currents of our lives into one harmonious surge of motion, we are able to say,

> Now rest my long, divided heart;
> Fixed on His blissful center, rest.

We should continue to pray with the Psalmist: "Unite my heart to sing Thy praise."

There was still another element in the contentment that the Apostle enjoyed in his Roman prison.

"I felt as if I were Siamese twins, one of which would have to die in order that the other might live."

Gertrude Behanna, *The Late Liz*

Psalm 86:11

83

Probably it was to this element that he directly referred. In Christ also he found *the rest of adequate resources*. Just after the mention of initiation into a secret he made a truly magnificent declaration, "I can do all things through Christ Who strengtheneth me." The full force of his words comes out better in the rendering, "I am strong for anything in Him Who makes me able." In Christ Paul felt strong for anything!

Competency to deal with things as they arise and the confidence that goes with it are essential to serenity.

It has been said that the art of living consists in the ability to say with meaning and sincerity I am, I ought, I can, I will. A sense of the mystery of being, a recognition of obligations, a consciousness of power, strong determinations—these are the components of true living.

It is at the third point, the ability to say *I can*, that most of us break down. How often have I looked at a great railway engine, throbbing with suppressed power as it waited to commence its long journey, and asked myself whether I had equal efficiency for my own day's task? When we have a disabling sense of inadequacy, there is necessarily an absence of repose. Peace is largely a matter of reserves.

Paul faced life with an air of sublime confidence because he was conscious of possessing reserves adequate for meeting any situation whatsoever. His assertion is so remarkable that we should be quite clear about the nature of the power that made such poise possible.

It was not human power. No man, however strong in himself, would dare to say, "I can do all things."

It was not human power reinforced. We have heard of the soldier in Wellington's army who asked to be

---

Philippians 4:13

"And it is easy, even without being religious one's self, to understand this . . . And, indeed, how can it possibly fail to steady the nerves, to cool the fever, and appease the fret, if one be sensibly conscious that, no matter what one's difficulties for the moment may appear to be, one's life as a whole is in the keeping of a power whom one can absolutely trust."

William James,
Varieties of Religious Experience

allowed to grasp the Iron Duke's "all-conquering hand" before going on a dangerous mission. A magnetic personality can do much to brace the flagging morale of another.

But the power of which Paul spoke was more than that. It was nothing less than Christ's own power communicated to him and into him through the medium of mystic union. We might translate still more accurately: "I am strong for anything in Him Who infuses strength into me."

Christ's own strength within me! I see the Man of Nazareth moving from task to task in a great calm that was never disturbed. He knew no defeat. He was never thrown off balance. In one day He was confronted successively with a raging sea, a raving demoniac, a disease that no man could heal, and finally with death itself. He was equal to everything.

The power that made Him competent for His tasks is available to make me competent for mine. Should I not live in Union with Him and use the power? Then I, too, shall have the rest of adequate resources.

8

The Ordering of a Restful Day

"Surely in vain do they bustle about" (Psalm 39:6, Rotherham).

8

And let our ordered lives
Confess the beauty of Thy peace.

ORDER and the beauty of peace go together. The
fair flower of peace does not grow among the
weeds of an ill-regulated life. The radiance of a deep
inner serenity is the product of disciplining both in
the heart and in outward affairs. So we must think
together about the ordering of life in the interests of
serenity.

It must be a day by day ordering. It is wise to
regard each day as a life in itself, a life coming, as if by
birth, out of the mystery of the dawn, running its
appointed course, and then sinking into the death of
sleep. What we call our life is but a succession of
thousands of these little lives. How important is it,
therefore, that each one should be ordered aright.

We have arrived at the stage when all that we have
been considering (about rest) should be brought to
the focal point of each day's living. *Do something
about it*. Resolve upon it now. Then learn how to-
morrow may be an ordered day confessing the beauty
of God's peace. I make definite suggestions about
ordering a day for rest.

Attend first to *the opening of the day*. The opening
should be ordered so that one may move restfully
into the day.

THE ORDERING OF
A RESTFUL DAY

Do not rush into the day. Rush cannot live together with rest. The day which begins with rush will most likely continue with rush. Let the first minutes of the wakening day be spent in an atmosphere of quiet leisureliness.

At once meet with your Lord. He is waiting for you in the inner sanctuary. It is good to devote your first waking thoughts to the recollection of God. Do you remember that on the evening of the day of resurrection Jesus appeared to the disciples, standing in the midst and saying, "Peace be unto you"; and that the record adds significantly, "But Thomas, one of the twelve, called Didymus, was not with them when Jesus came"?

Thomas missed Jesus and His benediction of peace! Let us not, in the morning hour, make a similar mistake. In the diary of Dr. Chalmers there occur repeatedly entries such as this: "Began my first waking minutes with a confident hold of Christ as my Savior. A day of great quietness."

I suggest that there be a morning act of faith. The will is central in the life of the spirit. To secure a healthy activity of the will in the first hour is to be well on the way to the sort of day one hopes to enjoy. Get the will functioning early. I suggest a morning act of faith such as this:

I believe that with Christ living within me through the Holy Spirit, recognized, trusted and obeyed, my life today can be happy, restful and strong. Deliberately I surrender my life to Him and trust Him to do the mighty work within of cleansing and empowering.

I believe also that God will manage my affairs today if I hand over the control to Him. I do that now and refuse to take anything back into my own care.

In this faith I go out into the day with quietness and confidence as my strength.

You may prefer a shorter statement which could be committed easily to memory and repeated throughout the day.

I am concerned to make clear that the Christian life is a matter of multiplied new beginnings. Every morning may be, and should be, the occasion of a new departure. "Hast thou," asked the Patriarch Job, "commanded the morning, and caused the dayspring to know its place?" By commencing the day with God, we can become its Master and enter into true possession of it.

Mastery of the day also involves planning it aright.

It must be a purposeful day if it is to be tranquil. We should control our day and not be borne along, willy nilly, by it. It is for us to choose, in large degree, what it will contain.

Again I offer practical suggestions.

The hours should be planned. To plan time is to have more time. Great serene souls never complain about not having time. They work steadily and quietly to a plan.

Dr. Alexander Whyte was insistent that we have plenty of time for all our work: Said he to fellow ministers, "We cannot look into one another's faces and say it is want of time. It is want of intention. It is want of determination. It is want of method. It is want of motive. It is want of conscience. It is want of heart. It is want of anything and everything but time." But the planning must be wise. The day should be spaced out according to basic duties and not be overburdened with things irrelevant to one's life purpose.

"The perseverance of the saints consists in ever new beginnings."

Alexander Whyte

THE ORDERING OF
A RESTFUL DAY

One can profit greatly from the advice given by Fenelon to the Duc de Chevreuse, whose inner life of prayer was being spoilt by pressure of duties. The Duke was told to observe the method of the wise gardener who carefully sees to it that the young trees have sufficient spaces one from the other in which to grow and expand. In the same way Fenelon advised the "racketed" and distracted nobleman to choose carefully between competing claims so that he would succeed in placing each action within a "circumambient air of leisure," of leisure for the spirit of prayer and peace. *Proper spacing and around each duty an air of leisure.* Do you see the idea?

Three disciplines are necessary for the maintenance of tranquility throughout the day. The first is that of relaxation. Little of what we have been discussing can be translated into daily living unless we take ourselves sternly in hand and learn to relax. For some of us it may be necessary to take special means to achieve relaxation. Let those who have taut nerves make brief pauses in the day's work and deliberately, firmly, relax every muscle more and more until, as a medical authority has it, the rest trickles out of the fingertips. We should also learn to relax while we work by avoiding nervous movements, excitable, unrestrained speech and bodily tension. Remember that relaxation is necessary for a restful day.

Our second daily discipline has to do with joyousness. The Fathers used to speak of accidie, by which they meant the spirit of gloom; of listlessness; of discouragement, which often invades life with the accompaniment of cynicism, criticism and unkindliness. Those who fall prey to it have an air of indolence because nothing is more wearing than accidie.

We touch here on one of the most efficient causes of modern restlessness, especially among people of middle age. The Christian should regard it as an evil

"For the good are always the merry."

William Butler Yeats

spirit to be exorcised in the power of Christ. Francis of Assisi impressed upon his disciples that when a servant of God is prey to heaviness, he ought, at once, to humble himself before God in prayer and remain in all humility before his Father until he finds again "the joy of his salvation." Cast out accidie and in Clement of Alexandria's great phrase, "anoint yourself with the perennial immortal bloom of gladness." The restful day must be a happy day.

"She was one of God's merry saints."

The third discipline relates to worry. Paul has already shown us the way out of worry. When the Lord Jesus said, "Be not anxious for your life," He used a word which describes the state of mind of one who is drawn in different directions. We have seen how Paul overcame such inner derangement by a wholehearted surrender to the will of the Sovereign Christ.

Make a discipline of the instruction. Take definite action about your worry. Tell yourself that it is futile and wasteful and even evil because it denies the care of the Heavenly Father. Then surrender yourself *with your worries* to Christ. What we cannot do with the curse of a worrying nature, Christ can.

—Plus accepting interruptions as from God (see p. 46).

The restful day must be a carefree day. When these three disciplines are observed, the course of the day is well ordered for rest.

I make some suggestions as to how *the close* of the day may best be used for rest. The vesper hour is God's appointed time for spiritual culture.

This is the best opportunity for self-examination. In the heart of the family circle we know ourselves better than elsewhere. Search the heart for causes of unrest, more especially for resentments. "Never go to bed angry," said Paul.

At eventide we should learn to go to God with our tiredness. How willingly the mother receives the weary child who creeps nearer and nearer until it

93

nestles in her arms. God's children become tired, too, so tired that they cannot often pray in formal language. God understands. Jesus was often tired. There is a sympathetic Heart that waits to receive our weariness and to enfold us in love.

The day should close finally with sleep that is truly a rest in the Lord: Some of us need very much to learn how to sleep. God gives to His beloved in their sleep only when they are relaxed through and through, by consciously resting in Him.

Go to sleep with some great divine word filling heart and mind, and God will bless you even in the hours of unconsciousness.

And what if sleep eludes one?

"What helped me to pass wakeful hours," said one of the men of the Knotted Heart, "was just remembering the Insomnia of God:

> Behold He that keepeth Israel
> He slumbers not, nor sleeps."

Epilogue

SOME TIME ago I traveled by air to New Zealand. As we drew near to our destination, morning began to break. With the eastern sky a blaze of glory I thrilled to think that I *was going into the dawn.*

Already the sun had made of the clouds beneath a glistening snowfield through which, far below, the blue ocean could be seen. Already, too, the wings of the plane were shining like polished silver. Then another touch was added to the exquisite beauty of the morning. The rays of the sun had become stronger and now transmuted the whirling hubs of the propellers into pure gold.

The dawn was coming out to me. I was going into the dawn. Could I help thinking of another dawn when the "flaming of Christ's advent feet" will fill the sky? The dawn was coming out to me. Could I help thinking of the radiance which, even now, streams from on high into hearts that love His appearing?

We who seek serenity should remind ourselves that our desire will never be entirely fulfilled in time. Our earthbound setting does not permit of the complete satisfying of the soul which is created in the likeness of the immortal God. But, for our great comfort, let us ever remember that we are going into the dawning of a day in which a perfect vision, a perfect life and a perfect home will meet every last need of the questing soul.

What a prospect! *A perfect vision.* In that glad dawning the Sunrising from on high will not only appear, but will also be fully unveiled. We shall see the King in His beauty "without a veil between." *A perfect life.* "When we shall see Him we shall be like Him, for we shall see Him as He is." *A perfect home,* a Father's house with many mansions in which there is room enough for us all. And which we shall share with Christ.

We go into a dawn beyond which lies that final provision for our rest. And while we wait, the dawn comes out to us. All this is of Christ the Divine Rest Giver before Whom we bow in a closing act of worship.

This hath He done and shall we not adore Him?
  This shall He do and can we still despair?
Come let us quickly fling ourselves before Him,
  Cast at His feet the burthen of our care.

Yea thro' life, death, thro' sorrow and thro'
    sinning
  He shall suffice me, for He hath sufficed:
Christ is the end, for Christ was the beginning,
  Christ the beginning, for the end is Christ.

Lines found in Mr. George Goodman's Bible written during his last illness (a mental breakdown):

"He led me by a way of pain
A barren and a starless place;
(I did not know His eyes were
    wet
He would not let me see His
    face.)
He left me like a frightened child
Unshielded in the night of
    storm,
(How should I dream He was so
    near?
The rainswept darkness hid His
    form.)
But when the clouds were
    drifting back
And dawn was breaking into day
I knew Whose feet had walked
    with mine
I saw His footprints all the way."

Date Due